OREGON

OREGON

Willard Clay & Larry Ulrich

with an introduction by
Kathy Clay

Sammamish Press

Will and Kathy Clay wish to thank Jim
and Carol Hammett for their valuable
assistance in photographing Oregon, and
to dedicate their work on this book to
Alton C. Elwood, their dear friend.

NEIL GOLDSCHMIDT
GOVERNOR

OFFICE OF THE GOVERNOR
STATE CAPITOL
SALEM, OREGON 97310-1347

Greetings:

As Governor of Oregon, I am proud to be a part of this photographic tribute to our state. This volume will give you an opportunity to see the splendor of the Oregon landscape, and, perhaps, to understand how Oregonians feel about their state.

Oregonians are very proud of the beauty and diversity of their state. The rugged coast line, the stately mountains, the fertile and verdant Willamette Valley, and the starkly majestic high desert region are all equally beautiful and radically diverse.

Through these photographs one can understand the attraction that the Oregon landscape had for the first pioneers who settled here. Here was land in which they could build a life, both breathtakingly beautiful and capable of supporting their families for generations. Oregonians feel a deep commitment to the legacy they inherited from the first settlers, and a need to extend that commitment into the future by preserving its beauty while maintaining an eye toward the progress of the state.

I hope that through these photographs you will begin to love Oregon as I do. I extend my warmest invitation to see these sights through your own eyes. We Oregonians love our state and are happy to share it with you. Enjoy your "voyage" through this book.

Warmest regards,

Neil Goldschmidt
Governor

INTRODUCTION

I sit on a bluff overlooking the mighty Pacific ocean. It is a beautiful day, the first after a week of gray sky and rain. Above me gulls float on a strong westerly wind. Below the waves crash against the rocks with the incoming tide. The coast guard buoys drone their lonesome cry and I am hypnotized by the entire scene. I will sit here for hours watching the gulls, taking deep breaths of ocean air, not really thinking of much. It is a spiritual experience. I find immense contentment in being here and look forward to returning even before I leave.

This is what most people come to see, the miles and miles of coastline protected from man's private buildings, belonging to all who want to partake of its beauty. Oregon has more miles of protected public coastal land than any other continental state and the scenery is as varied as the number of places to see. From the sea stacks at Cannon Beach to the long sandy beaches of the Oregon Dunes, the coast holds treasures for all.

This afternoon there will be a very low tide and the beach will be busy with treasure hunters. I will return here to watch them from above on my bluff perch. They look for polished agates, tide pools full of color and life, pieces of sculptured driftwood. Some have buckets and dig for the elusive razor clam, others take the more productive approach and pull the now exposed mussels off their rock homes. A few, like me, have come to sit and stare at the ocean, allowing themselves to become captivated by such an awesome sight of waves and endless sea.

But Oregon is not just a state with a beautiful coastline. It is a state of incredible diversity. Less than one hundred miles from the coast rise the foothills of the Cascade Range. This range separates the state into two areas completely opposite from one another; one wet and plant-covered, the other dry and sparse. Warm wet air blowing in from the ocean hits the wall of the Cascade Range and is forced up to where it cools. Clouds form and soon drop their moisture on the west side of the range. Heavy rainfall on the west of the Cascades contrasts with semi-desert aridity to the east. A dramatic difference on account of a dramatic mountain range.

Along the Cascade Range old volcanic peaks rise up to elevations of 10,000 feet above sea level. Although at 11,329 feet it is not the nation's highest peak, Mt. Hood's perfect summit rises sheer from relatively lowlying land. Like the ocean, Mt. Hood overwhelms the mind. Its huge mass is simply hard to comprehend.

Other peaks share this range; Mt. Bachelor, The Three Sisters, Broken Top, Mt. Jefferson, Mt. Thielsen, Mt. Scott and Mt. McLoughlin. All are impressive, all are beautifully covered with snow in the winter and several have some of the best skiing slopes in the United States. During the warmer months, hikers enjoy the cool alpine trails, fish in the lakes, and eat wild blueberries in late summer. There are not many experiences that compare with spending a night camped in a tent below Mt. Jefferson, listening to the boulders falling down this eroding mountain.

Oregon's one and only national park lies in the southern portion of the Cascade Range. Crater Lake formed thousands of years ago after Mount Mazama, a 15,000 foot volcano, erupted and blew out so much of the mountain's mass that there was no support left for the surrounding walls. They collapsed, creating the caldera, which eventually filled with rain, snow, and spring water to make what is now, at 1932 feet, the deepest lake in the United States. Its unforgettably intense color is a reflection of the sky above. On a clear day it is the most beautiful indigo blue imaginable.

The majority of Oregon's land lies east of the Cascade Range. Here the ponderosa pine grows in the dry forests, farm land is irrigated, and cattle are grazed on range predominantly covered with sage brush. The native Oregonians' faces are weathered from hot dry summers and cold frigid winters. Where moisture had so much to do with the landscape and its inhabitants west of the Cascades, here dryness shapes and molds the land and its people, creating a totally unique beauty, so different as to defy comparison with that of western Oregon, rather a beauty that stands on its own.

Along the Columbia River northern Oregon is covered with tilled acres of wheat and alfalfa. Over rolling hills and flat land, square fields and round fields make a beautiful patchwork of shapes and colors during the entire year. Small towns are spread out miles from each other and the "True West" feeling is strong. Pendleton hosts an annual rodeo that draws cowboys, rodeo enthusiasts, and tourists from miles away.

But the cultivation must stop at the slopes of the Wallowa Mountains. Here the pristine Eagle Cap Wilderness has been preserved so that nature may continue without the threat of chainsaws, roads, or buildings. Wallowa Lake, a natural glacier-made lake, lies at the entrance to this wilderness area and on a calm day reflects a mountain range that some have called "The Little Swiss Alps". A good trail leads hikers to Glacier Pass, 12 miles within the wilderness, for a breathtaking and breathcatching view of Glacier Lake, clear and clean and blue.

The Snake River marks the upper half of the eastern boundary of Oregon. Its waters flow north roaring over rapids in Hells Canyon which at 8,000 feet is the deepest gorge in North America. Leaving the state south of Ontario, the Snake takes water from the Owyhee River, a newly dedicated wild and scenic river, a river that works its way through some of the most wild and beautiful desert terrain of Oregon.

Here too in this unpopulated southeastern section of Oregon is an oasis in the desert—the Malheur National Wildlife Refuge, a major resting, nesting, and feeding area on the Pacific Flyway, for trumpeter swans, sandhill cranes, bald eagles and numerous other bird and wildlife species. The Refuge's three lakes are supplied with water from streams which originate in the surrounding mountains. One of these rivers, the Blitzen River, flows north from Steens Mountain through the Blitzen Valley before reaching Malheur Lake.

About 100 miles north of Malheur lies John Day Fossil Beds National Monument, preserved to protect its valuable scientific resource—fossils. In protecting the fossils, much beautiful scenery has also been preserved. Saved from motor bikes and sand buggies, the dramatically eroded landscape of volcanic ash at Painted Hills is a national monument. Its mineral-bearing clays seem to glow at sunrise and sunset. Sheep Rock stands above the John Day River, whose waters carry eroded sand and silt across miles and miles of Oregon terrain to dump them finally into the Columbia Gorge over two hundred miles away.

Not too far off is the largest Indian reservation in Oregon, the Warm Springs Indian Reservation. The Deschutes River marks its eastern border and is, in my opinion, Oregon's most beautiful river. Fishermen and rafters float down this river in flat-bottomed drift boats and rubber rafts, letting the current decide how fast they will travel. They camp along the river's edge, listening to its music and eating its delicious rainbow trout. Although there is plenty of water in the river, campfires are restricted because the surrounding land is parched and tinder dry. The days are hot, the nights are cool, and the water is ice cold. The Deschutes empties its silt and sand into the Columbia Gorge, to be carried off to the Pacific Ocean.

And again, I have returned to the ocean. The sun is now setting, backlighting the waves as they topple over themselves. A flock of pelicans moves south, on to a resting place for the night. Almost everyone has gone from the beach now, gone home to study their treasures or eat their clams and mussels. However different from most of the state, the ocean is a symbol of Oregon—a place for discoveries, a place for meditation, diverse and varied, beautiful in so many ways.

KATHY CLAY

1 (*right*) View of the Oregon coast south from Cascade Head Natural Area near Lincoln City; Siuslaw National Forest.

2 (*overleaf*) Downtown Portland from the Rose Gardens.

3 Oneonta Gorge, Columbia River.

4 (*right*) Grande Ronde Valley from Mt. Emily.

5 Farming in the northwest; (*left*) dairy farm near Tillamook and (*right*)
winter wheat in the Tualatin Valley.

6 Clearing storm at sunset over Haystack Rock; Cape Kiwanda State Park.

7 (*right*) Reflection of moonrise over The Sisters at Scott Lake; Willamette National Forest.

8 (*left*) Afternoon light on rocky beach and Yaquina Lighthouse near Newport; Agate Beach State Park.

9 Icebergs in a lake below Bend Glacier at Broken Top; Three Sisters Wilderness.

10 (*left*) Sahalie Falls, McKenzie River; Willamette National Forest.

11 Old abandoned ranch house near Maupin; Wasco County.

12 (*left*) Ramona Falls in the Mt. Hood Wilderness below Mt. Hood; Mt. Hood National Forest.

13 Multnomah Falls, Columbia River Gorge; Mt. Hood National Forest.

14 (*left*) Maple trees in fall color below Mt. Jefferson; Mt. Jefferson Wilderness.

15 Mushrooms and maple leaves on moss-covered lava boulders near McKenzie Pass; Three Sisters Wilderness.

16 (*left*) Cape Lookout from Netarts Bay.

17 Morning light on farm buildings along the Sunset Highway
(Highway 26); Willamette Valley.

18 (*left*) Evening light and low tide surf on sandstone cliffs; Cape Kiwanda State Park.

19 Wheatfields near Summerville; Grande Ronde Valley.

20 Heceta Head Lighthouse.

21 (*right*) Mt. Jefferson from Jefferson Park;
Mt. Jefferson Wilderness.

22 Coastline south of Cape Perpetua.

23 (*right*) Waterfront at Garibaldi;
Tillamook Bay.

24 Mt. Hood National Forest; (*left*) mushrooms and bunchberries in the fall, and (*right*) coniferous forest in winter.

25 (*overleaf*) Winter morning light on snow-covered Bachelor Butte near Bend; Deschutes National Forest.

26 High tide in sunset light on sea stack below Tillamook Lighthouse;
Cape Meares State Park.

27 (*right*) Sunset glow on Mt. Jefferson; Mt. Jefferson Wilderness.

28 (*left*) Cape Kiwanda and Haystack Rock.

29 Rolled hay in Warner Valley, Warner Peak in the distance; Lake County.

30 (*left*) Rocky shore and fall color along Breitenbush River near Detroit; Willamette National Forest.

31 The Crooked River; Smith Rock State Park.

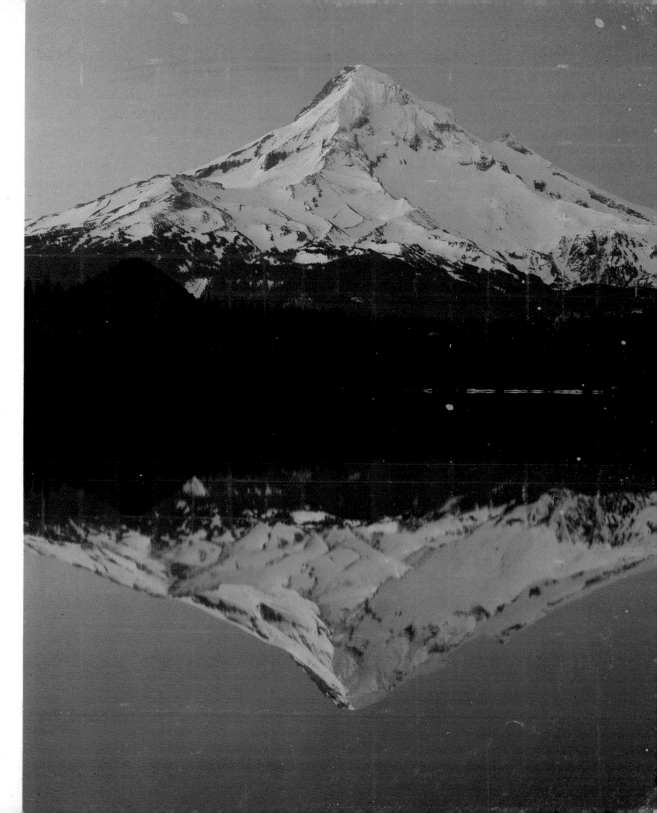

32 (*left*) Light breaking through storm at Heceta Head Lighthouse; Devil's Elbow State Park.

33 Sunrise light on Mt. Hood reflected in Lost Lake; Mt. Hood National Forest.

34 Hiker dwarfed by 93 ft. Lower South Falls; Silver Falls State Park.

35 (*right*) Tunnel Falls, Eagle Creek Trail; Columbia River Gorge.

36 Arrowleaf balsam root in a field of golden alexanders in the Blue
Mountains; Umatilla County.

37 (*right*) Morning light and clearing storm over ranch below the
Wallowa Mountains; Joseph.

38 (*left*) View of Strawberry Lake from near summit of Strawberry Mt., Strawberry Mountain Wilderness; Malheur National Forest.

39 Eagle Cap Mt. from tarn near Horton Pass; Eagle Cap Wilderness.

40 Mirror Lake, Wallowa Mts.; Eagle Cap Wilderness.

41 (*right*) Matterhorn; Eagle Cap Wilderness.

42 Fox.

43 (*right*) Strawberry Mt. from John Day River Valley; near Prairie City.

44 Cant Ranch and Sheep Rock; John Day Fossil Beds National
Monument.

45 (*right*) Historic mining town of Granite; Blue Mts.

46 Moss-covered rocks below Strawberry
Falls, Strawberry Mountain Wilderness;
Malheur National Forest.

47 (*right*) Orchard of pear trees at Parkdale
below snow-capped Mt. Hood; Hood River
County.

48 Pioneer buildings; (*left*) old barn and fence on Sigford Ranch along
Highway 26 near Mitchell, Wheeler County and (*right*) Fort Clatsop
National Memorial, Astoria.

49 John Day Fossil Beds National Monument; (*left*) The Painted Hills and (*right*) stand of Beeplant (*cleome platycarpa*) in clay mound ravines.

50 John Day River; (*left*) evening light on rock formations along Rock Creek and (*right*) evening light below Sheep Rock.

51 (*overleaf*) Rainbow over juniper woodland; John Day River Country.

52 (*left*) Moonrise and sunset light over the prairie; Hart Mt. National Antelope Refuge

53 Mule deer tracks and frosted junipers; Drinkwater Pass near Drewsey.

54 Steens Mountain; (*left*) Alvord Desert from East Rim Viewpoint, and (*right*) aspen grove in Whorehouse Meadow.

55 (*overleaf*) Sunset on the high desert of southeastern Oregon.

56 Eroded lava-rock formations in Leslie Gulch; Mahogany Mts.

57 (*right*) View of Owyhee River winding through Owyhee Canyon
near Three Forks; Jordan Valley.

58 (*left*) Trees covered with hoar frost along the Snake River near Ontario; Ontario State Park.

59 Abert Rim from Abert Lake.

60 (*left*) Stand of teasel and grasses along the shore of Benson Pond;
Malheur National Wildlife Refuge.

61 Summer storm clouds over maze of waterways at Lower Campbell
Lake; Hart Mt. National Antelope Refuge.

62 Umpqua scenic dunes; Oregon Dunes
National Recreation Area.

63 (*right*) Sand patterns on the sand dunes
near the Pacific Ocean; Oregon Dunes
National Recreation Area.

64 Paradise Lost Room; Oregon Caves
National Monument.

65 (*right*) Sunset at Bandon Beach.

66 (*left*) Sunrise light on weathered pier pilings and Coquille River
Lighthouse; Bandon Beach.

67 Charleston Harbor, Coos Bay.

68 Historic buildings; (*left*) the mining town of Granite, in the Blue Mountains, and (*right*) California Street in Jacksonville.

69 (*overleaf*) Storm clouds and rabbit bush; Fort Rock State Park.

70 (*left*) Rhododendrons on the Siltcoos sand dunes; Oregon Dunes
National Recreation Area.

71 Cape Arago Lighthouse from Sunset Bay State Park.

72 Lemolo Falls, North Umpqua River.

73 (*right*) Cape Sebastian and Hunters Island.

74 Incense cedar, Grasshopper Meadow; Rogue-Umpqua Divide Wilderness.

75 (*right*) View down Little Blitzen Gorge from near the summit; Steens Mt.

76 Dogwood in bloom below Mill Creek
Falls on the Rogue River; Rogue River
National Forest.

77 Rhododendrons around the pond of Oriental Garden; Botanical
Gardens, Shore Acres State Park.

78 (*left*) Crashing waves on eroded rock formations on Simpson Beach;
Shore Acres State Park.

79 Lichen-covered boulders and storm clouds over Coyote Hills in southern Oregon; Valley Falls.

80 (*left*) Winter sunset light on Broken Top in the Cascade Range; Deschutes National Forest.

81 Lifting storm over Phantom Ship seen from Sun Notch; Crater Lake National Park.

82 Evening light through lifting storm on rabbit bush near Cleetwood
Trail; Crater Lake National Park.

83 (*right*) Islands and shoreline around Wizard Island as viewed from
near The Watchman; Crater Lake National Park.

84 (*left*) Winter sunrise light on Wizard Island and Crater Lake; Crater Lake National Park.

85 Winter morning light on snow-encrusted coniferous trees; Crater Lake National Park.

86 Winter storm and evening light over Crescent Beach; Ecola State Park.

87 (*right*) Coquille River Lighthouse at sunset; Bandon.

88 Rocks and logs at low tide; Harris Beach State Park.

89 (*right*) Low tide on Crescent Beach; Ecola State Park.

90 Sunset and rock formations at low tide; Bandon Beach.

91 (*right*) Sunset at low tide below Goat Island (part of the National
Wildlife Refuge system); Harris Beach State Park.

92 Heceta Head Lighthouse.

93 (*overleaf*) Wizard Island at sunrise; Crater Lake National Park.

94 Haystack Rock from the beach at Pacific City.

PHOTOGRAPHIC CREDITS